Ruby and the Rubbish Bin

Margot Sunderland

Illustrated by

Nicky Armstrong

Routledge
Taylor & Francis Group

LONDON AND NEW YORK

Helping Children with Feelings Series
Storybook & Guidebook Sets

Using Story-telling as a Therapeutic Tool with Children ISBN 978 0 86388 425 2
Willy and the Wobbly House ISBN 978 0 86388 498 6
Helping Children who are Anxious or Obsessional ISBN 978 0 86388 454 2
A Wibble Called Bipley (and a few Honks) ISBN 978 0 86388 494 8
Helping Children who have Hardened their Hearts or Become Bullies ISBN 978 0 86388 458 0
A Pea Called Mildred ISBN 978 0 86388 497 9
Helping Children Pursue Their Hopes and Dreams ISBN 978 0 86388 455 9
A Nifflenoo Called Nevermind ISBN 978 0 86388 496 2
Helping Children who Bottle Up Their Feelings ISBN 978 0 86388 457 3
The Frog who Longed for the Moon to Smile ISBN 978 0 86388 495 5
Helping Children who Yearn for Someone They Love ISBN 978 0 86388 456 6
Teenie Weenie in a Too Big World ISBN 978 0 86388 460 3
Helping Children with Fear ISBN 978 0 86388 464 1
How Hattie Hated Kindness ISBN 978 0 86388 461 0
Helping Children Locked in Rage or Hate ISBN 978 0 86388 465 8
Ruby and the Rubbish Bin ISBN 978 0 86388 462 7
Helping Children with Low Self-Esteem ISBN 978 0 86388 466 5
The Day the Sea Went Out and Never Came Back ISBN 978 0 86388 463 4
Helping Children with Loss ISBN 978 0 86388 467 2

First published 2003 by Speechmark Publishing Ltd.

Published 2017 by Routledge

2 Park Square, Milton Park, Abingdon, Oxon OX14 4RN

711 Third Avenue, New York, NY 10017, USA

Routledge is an imprint of the Taylor & Francis Group, an informa business

Text copyright © M Sunderland 2003
Illustrations copyright © N Armstrong 2003

British Library Cataloguing in Publication Data
Sunderland, Margot
Ruby and the rubbish bin: a story for children with low self-esteem. – (Helping children with feelings)
1. Self-esteem – Juvenile fiction.
2. Friendship – Juvenile fiction.
3. Children's stories
I. Title II. Armstrong, Nicky
823.9'14 (J)

ISBN 978-0-863-88462-7 (pbk)

Printed in the UK by Severn, Gloucester on responsibly sourced paper

Once, there was a little girl called Ruby.

The trouble was . . .
Ruby felt more like a piece of rubbish than a little girl.

Sometimes she felt like something you find in a bin.

Sometimes she felt like something on the pavement that people stand on.

Children in the playground shouted, "Ruby rubbish!"

Big bully boys yelled from the bus, "Stupid-girly-whirly hair." They even dropped their ice-cream wrappers on Ruby's head.

And one of Ruby's teachers, Mrs Fruity-Nose, often picked on Ruby. She told Ruby that she wasn't sitting up straight, wasn't being neat enough, and that she had to try a lot harder.

When Ruby drew a house, she said to herself, "It's a rubbish house," and she scribbled it out. When Ruby drew a tree, she said to herself, "It's a rubbish tree," and she threw it away.

And when Ruby looked at herself in the mirror, she saw a yukky, smelly girl. "You're so ugly," thought Ruby.

After school, Ruby liked hanging around the rubbish bins. She didn't know why she liked it. She just did. Sometimes she even felt like getting into one of the bins and never coming out.

Each Friday, the dustbin men came to empty the rubbish from the bins.

"Hello, sweetie!" said one of them. "I'm not a sweetie," said Ruby, "I'm rubbish."

Each Saturday, Ruby went to the sweet shop to buy some sherbet lemons. "There you are, lovey," said the sweet-shop lady. "I'm not a lovey," said Ruby, "I'm rubbish."

And the last time she was there a little girl said, "I like your hair." "It's stupid-girly-whirly hair," said Ruby. "It's funny," she thought, "how people can get you so wrong."

One day, Ruby's Auntie Flo in Australia sent
Ruby some super red and black trainers.
Ruby thought they were great.

In fact, for the whole afternoon, Ruby didn't feel
rubbish at all. She really felt quite OK. People at
school liked her trainers too.

Now the problem with things like trainers is that they don't make you feel good about yourself for very long. And sure enough, when Ruby did her homework that evening and couldn't spell 'sausage' or 'spaghetti', it all came back. "I'm a rubbish speller," said Ruby, "I'm just rubbishy Ruby and that's all there is to it."

And at that moment, Ruby felt so rubbishy that she wanted to sleep and sleep and never wake up again.

Then one day at school, there was a new lunchtime lady called Dot. Dot had just moved into a house in the same street as Ruby.

When Ruby stood in the lunch queue, Dot smiled at Ruby. It was such a lovely smile, that something warm happened in Ruby's tummy.

In fact, Ruby was so surprised by the smile that she dropped her lunch.

"Oh dear, let me help you,"
said Dot the lunchtime lady.

Ruby was so surprised that Dot hadn't called her
'stupid' for dropping her lunch, that she dropped her
pudding too.

"Never mind, sweetheart," said Dot, putting her arm around Ruby. "It's funny how things can go wrong in twos, isn't it?"

Ruby tried to tell Dot that she wasn't a sweetheart, she was rubbish, but it didn't quite come out, because by then she had a big lump in her throat and wanted to cry.

On her way home, Ruby passed by Dot's house. Dot was sitting in her garden in a deck-chair. "Hey Ruby, I've got something for you," said Dot. To Ruby's surprise, Dot had drawn a picture of Ruby with lots of rubbish on her head. "Ruby, some of the nice teachers at school told me about how you think you are rubbish. Well now, I think you've got into a bit of a muddle."

"You see, when some people feel small, they try to make themselves feel big by making other people feel small instead. This is how bullies get made."

"But when it's you they pick on, it makes you feel you're rubbish."

Dot went on crossly, "And if people can't see how lovely you are, that's their loss, not yours."

Ruby didn't really understand this last bit, but it made the warm thing happen in her tummy again.

That night, Ruby had a dream . . .

In her dream, people were piling all sorts of rubbish over her head: stale chips, chewed up bits of pizza and smelly anchovies. Ruby was drowning in the rubbish, and then it got even more horrible because someone mistook Ruby for rubbish and put her in the bin too. It was awful.

But then something amazing happened. In her dream, Ruby suddenly felt very angry, and her anger made her feel so strong . . .

... that she poured the rubbish right back over everyone.

Next day in class, Mrs Fruity-Nose scolded Ruby for too many crossings out. Ted the Tough jeered at her for getting cheese sauce on her sweater, and someone called her stupid for wearing odd socks.

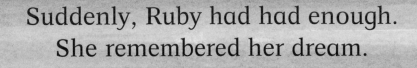

Suddenly, Ruby had had enough.
She remembered her dream.

She stood up. "Excuse me everybody, but let's get one thing straight from now on. I'm not rubbish. In fact, I'm getting really fed up with people who feel bad about themselves trying to make me feel bad instead."

"And if you can't see that I'm lovely, then it's your loss, not mine." Everyone clapped, except for the bullies, who fell over in shock, and Mrs Fruity-Nose, who looked very surprised indeed.

Ruby often visited Dot the lunchtime lady in her garden. They became great friends. Together they would do some gardening and laugh and talk.

It was so much fun, that sometimes it felt to Ruby as if they were flying together.

And when Dot smiled that special smile, or gave Ruby a little squeeze, Ruby felt like a princess.

And whenever Ruby went back to feeling rubbish, because of course she did from time to time . . .

. . . Dot would listen very carefully and help her to sort out her feelings so well, that the warm thing happened in Ruby's tummy again.

And after that, with her new friends, Ruby started visiting the little park at the end of her street. It was full of flowers and ponds.

"Not hanging around the rubbish any more?" asked the dustbin man as he walked by. "No, I prefer being here now," said Ruby, "it's so lovely."

"Just like you,"
said the dustbin man.
"Yes, just like me,"
said Ruby.